Fast Phonics Testimonials

This method for learning to read CLICKS and STICKS!
(Mrs. M., mother of 5, New Mexico)

My grandson did the cartoon letters in the car as I drove him to private school. When we arrived there, he wanted to CONTINUE practicing his phonics cartoons RATHER than go into his schoolroom! He's hooked!
(Mrs. F., grandmother of 9, Colorado)

Our first attempt at reading—using someone else's phonics program—came to a screeching halt. My daughter hated "learning to read." With this new approach her interest not only revived, she actually sat up and took ownership. She is now six and is teaching the cartoon letters to her four-year-old brother! (Mrs. H., mother of 4, New Mexico)

My older daughter of 6, when watching her younger sibling learn phonics with Mrs. Ellison's system, burst out with "Mom, if you had taught ME to read this way, I would have become a better reader!"
(Mrs. C., mother of 3, North Carolina)

With this method, my 3 and 1/2 year old learned all of her phonetic sounds in 4 days! And she retained them perfectly thereafter!
(Anne Green, mother of 3, Colorado)

The cartoon phonics system has been a blessing to our family. Because of the imagery connected with each letter, we were able to introduce phonics to our four-year-old and our two-year-old **at the same time**!
(Mrs. A, mother of 3, New Mexico)

Fast Phonics is FUN!

kite

ladder

mountain

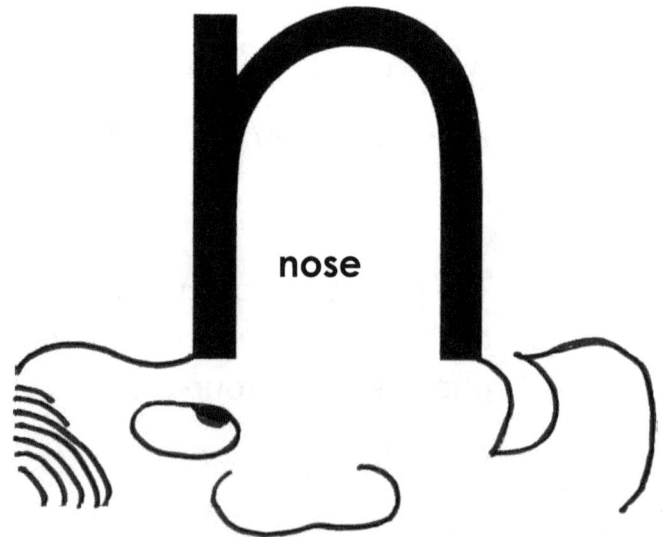

nose

...want to know the secret?

hat

dog

The phonetic SOUND is tucked into the letter SHAPE!

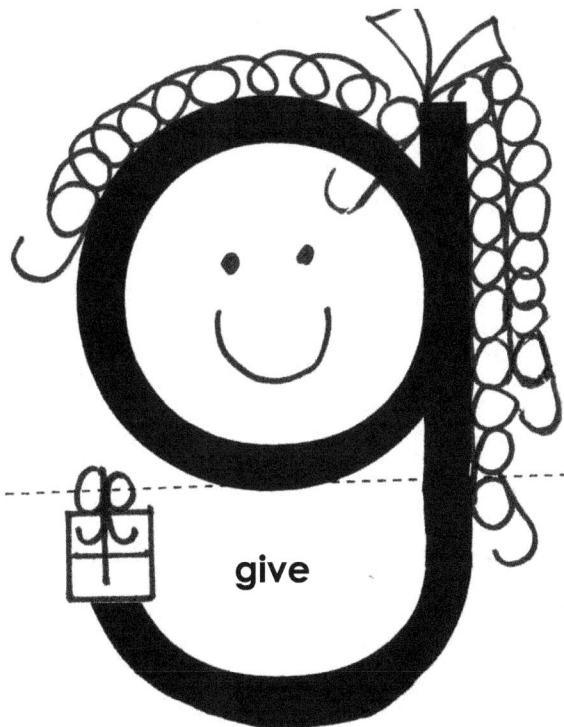

give

The results?

Lasting retention, right from the start.

A letter from Renée

Dear Parent/Teacher,

When undertaking any new endeavor, **beginnings are everything**. If foundations aren't secured well, the entire edifice can eventually collapse, given enough time and pressure. And so it is with reading instruction. Since reading is the first and most important academic challenge the child will ever undertake, it is of paramount importance that the process be handled with utmost care. It must end in success.

For an adult, reading can be a daily joy (as is the case with voracious readers) or a source of repeated embarrassment (as is the case with the functionally illiterate who live in a private daily nightmare). When the poor reader (we as a nation graduate millions of these) is forced to read aloud in public, all too often his halting, broken reading repeatedly dive-bombs his core identity and self-respect. And what we lose as a nation when a large percentage of our citizenry cannot comprehend basic instruction manuals, prescription drug cautions, insurance forms, public signage and application forms is incalculable.

Sadly, due to our poor reading instruction as a nation, for too long now, we sit below about 24 other countries in national reading scores. And this, from the most prosperous and progressive nation in the world.

Fast Phonics is now sent into the fray and chaos to help reverse all of this. It is a new solution to help halt our nation's academic downward spiral. This tightly designed advanced method succeeds in eliminating scores of possibilities for falling behind, or for suffering feelings of intimidation, or an inability to "keep up," or feelings of inferiority—even along the way. With *Fast Phonics*, "I CAN" is the child's constant companion. The student begins with "I DO read each new step" and ends up with "I can READ— I *get* this!"

You now have a tool in your hands that can help your loved ones, who have yet to learn to read, join the ranks of people who can read well and now can get there with remarkable speed.

Fast phonics letter cartoons

Fun for preschoolers, kindergartners and first graders

Renée Ellison

Intensive, systematic, phonics instruction would heal the bulk of our nation's illiteracy problem. The whole-word, "look-say" approach has been responsible for its demise.

(Summarized from the works of Dr. Samuel Blumenfeld, author of *The New Illiterates*)

Website: http://www.homeschoolhowtos.com
Email: info@homeschoolhowtos.com

Library of Congress Cataloging-in-Publication Data
Ellison, Renée R.
Fast phonics letter cartoons: Fun for preschoolers, kindergartners and first
    graders.
Durango, Colo.: Homeschool How-Tos, c2017.
48 p.
Teach faster series.
Reading (Elementary).
Reading-- Phonetic method-- Handbooks, manuals, etc.
Language arts (Elementary).
Home schooling-- Curricula.
Education-- Parent participation.
Home schooling-- Curricula-- United States-- Handbooks, manuals, etc.
LC classification (Partial): LB1573 .E   2017
ISBN: 978-0-9987894-1-5

Printed in the United States of America
Cover design by Erin Jones

How to use letter cartoons

Learn letter sounds easily with phonics cartoons. Why so easy?
Because the clue to the letter SOUND is hidden in the letter SHAPE.
The key to the letter is hidden in plain sight! Learning the correct
SOUND of letters, NOT their alphabet NAMES at first, eliminates
confusion and speeds up the reading process.

Learning these carefully crafted sound/symbol/letter cartoons gives
your child "right-now" first step success. These pictures create a
memory hook so strong that the child gains almost instant recall.
Captured by these whimsical letter images, children have begged to
do them again and again.

Day One:
Read the cartoons completely through, showing the child all of the
details of the cartoons. Read the phrase and say the isolated key
word (the trigger word) for each page. Follow the trigger word with
the first letter isolated phonetic sound. Say the sound 3X.
    Example: Apples hang on trees.   Apple.   "a", "a", "a"
Have the child say the trigger word and the phonetic sound right
after you, as an echo.

Day Two:
**Skip the phrase. Read only the trigger word and its isolated
phonetic sound, on each page.**
    Example: Apple.   "a", "a", "a"
Again, have the child say the trigger word and the phonetic sound
right after you, as an echo.

Day Three
This time say ONLY the isolated sound 3X.
   Example: "a", "a", "a".   Have the child echo you.

Skip the phrase and the word, entirely. Just as deliberately as you taught the phrase and word to the child (as memory hooks) you now want to wean the child off from them, so that he learns to see only the symbol and can reproduce its sound, without hesitation. From here on, say ONLY the phonetic sound every time you "read" the cartoons with the child.

Day Four and Beyond: Test phonetic sound recognition:
Begin to test the letters randomly, six at a time, by pointing to the plain letter charts of six letters and saying: "Which one says?" [Plain letter charts are found near the end of the book and have no dots or arrows on them.] To test, say the trigger word and its isolated phonetic sound until each set of six is known randomly. Then test again by ONLY saying the isolated phonetic sound. Do not move onto the next chart of six letters until the first six are known without hesitation.

Day Four and Beyond: No pencil tracing
On the **tracing** charts, found near the end of the book (they have starting dots and arrows), teach the child to trace the letter. Use your pointer finger to demonstrate how it is done while the child watches very carefully. Then have the child trace it using his own pointer finger. If the child is very young or can't get the hang of it, you can cup the child's fist in yours, with his pointer finger extended, and guide his hand FOR him in the proper direction of the arrows. Be sure to tap the starting dot in your demonstration of each one.

When the child knows the sounds and the tracing of all the letters, then teach him the two-letter words that follow.

apple

a

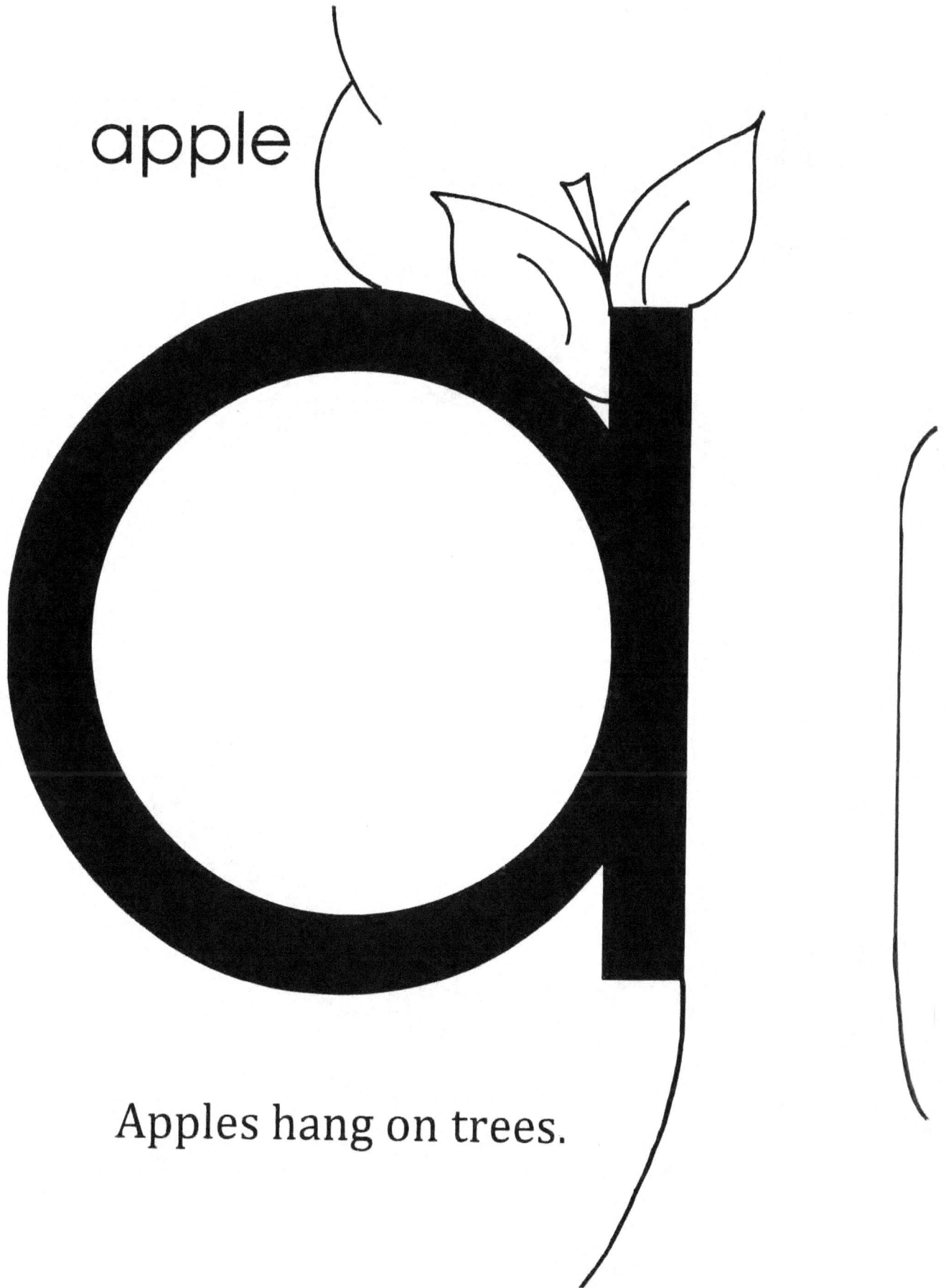

Apples hang on trees.

baby

b

Baby buggies bounce.

cat

Cats climb cleverly.

dog

Dogs despise doors.

elephant

Ellie, the elephant,
   munches on excellent eggs.

fix

f

saw

screwdriver

Fred fixes frames and furniture.

give

Gladys gives good gifts.

hat

Heidi hides under her hat

itch

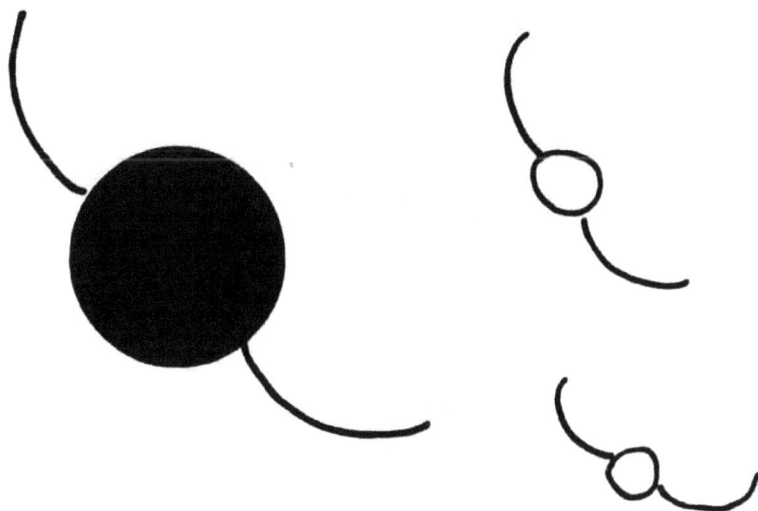

Icky mosquito bites itch.

jam

Jam the jelly in the jar.

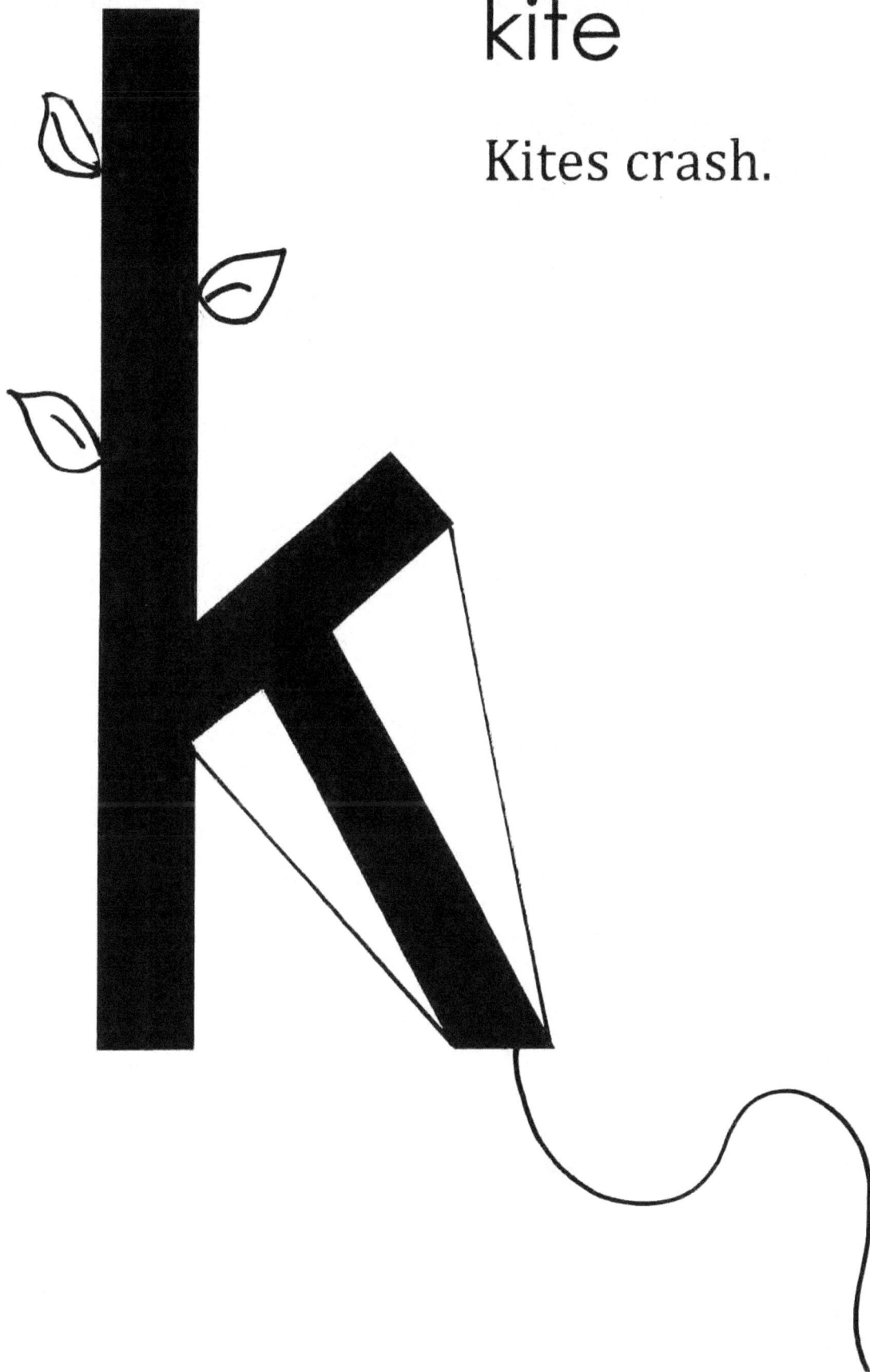

kite

Kites crash.

ladder

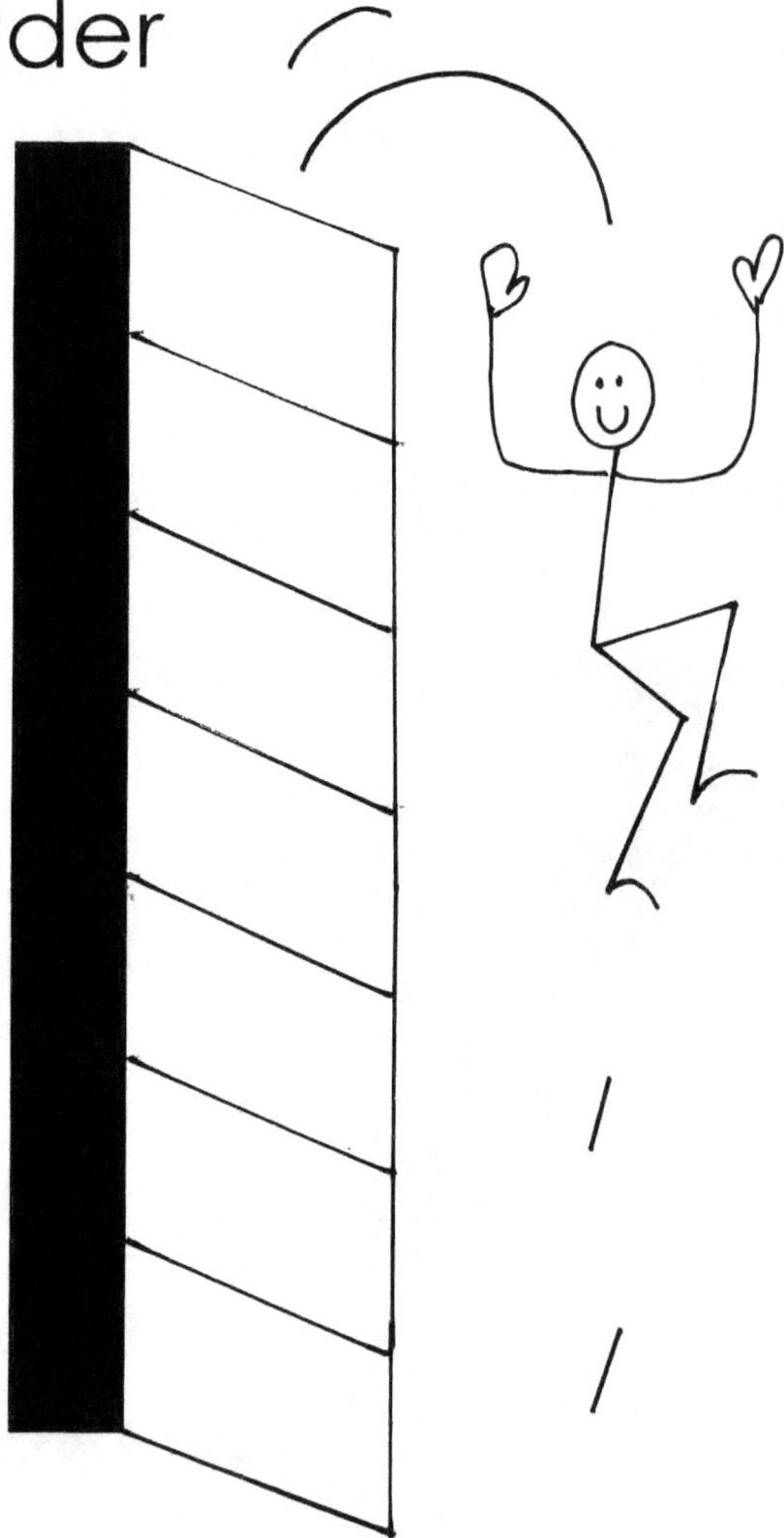

Larry loves ladder landings.

mountain

m

Mom motorcycles through the
mountains in the moonlight.

Ned's nose is not small.

nose

octopus

The odd octopus ogles oxygen.

pa

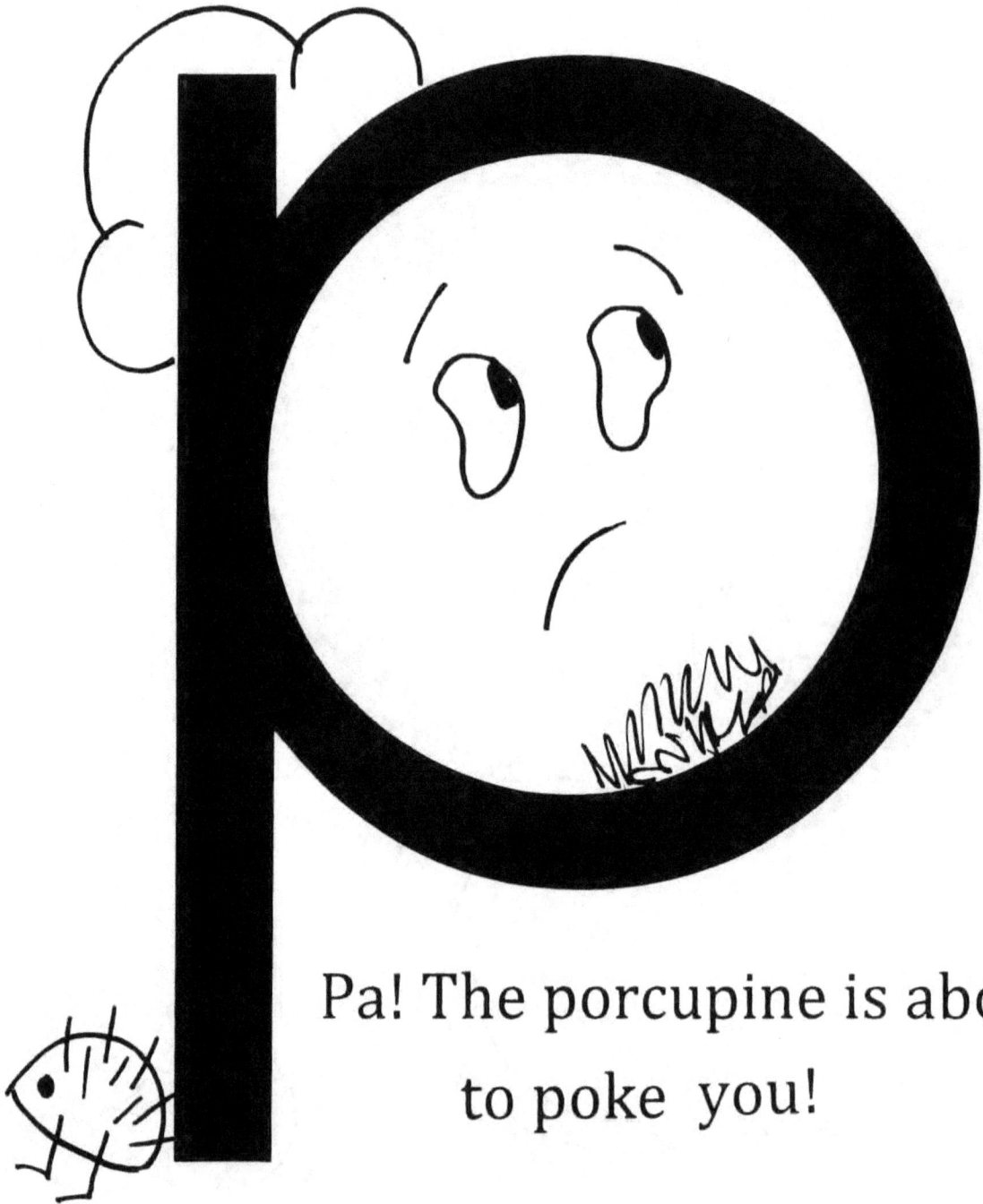

Pa! The porcupine is about
to poke you!

queen

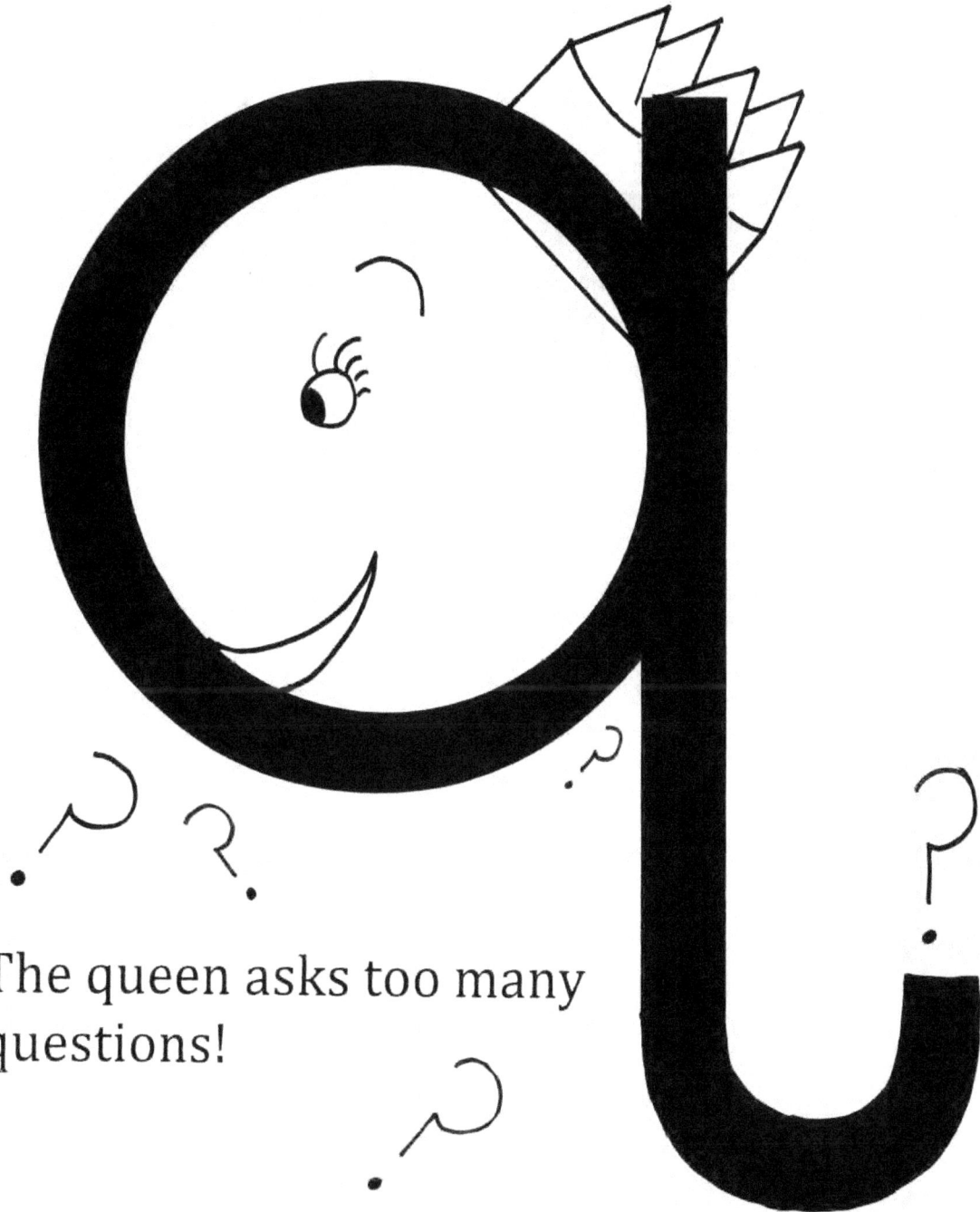

The queen asks too many questions!

ran

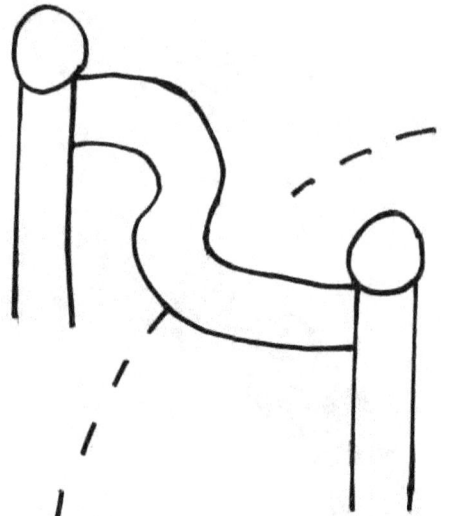

Rita ran the race and the crowd roared.

snake

Sam the snake slithers and smiles.

Tom

Tom talks tons.

up

Uppity up!

valley

Victory in the valley ! Vic saw no vipers!

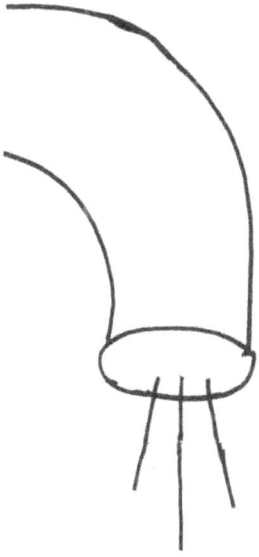

water

W

Water wanders.

ax

The ax attacks trees.

yes!
yo-yo's

Zebras walk in zig-zags.

Z

zebra

apple

baby

cat

dog

elephant

fix

cat

baby

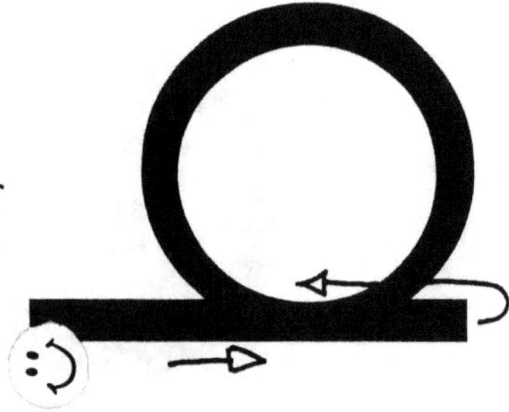

apple

fix

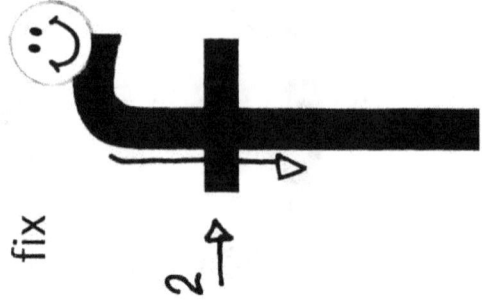

elephant

dog

itch

i

ladder

l

hat

h

kite

k

give

g

jam

j

itch

hat

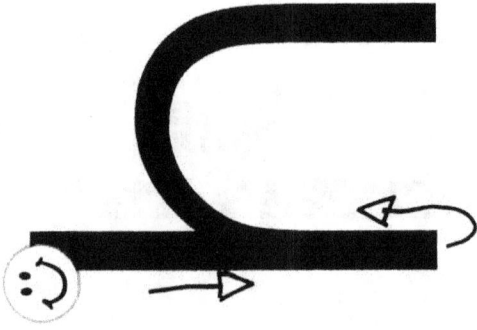

give

ladder

kite

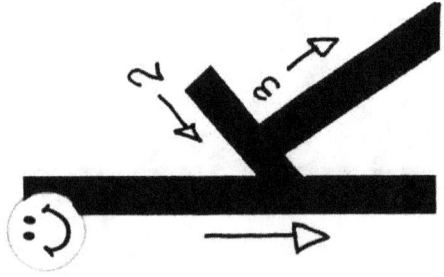

jam

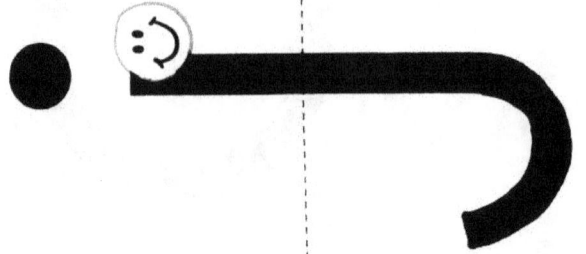

octopus

o

nose

n

mountain

m

ran

r

queen

q

pa

p

octopus

nose

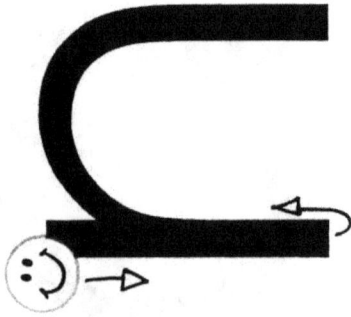

mountain

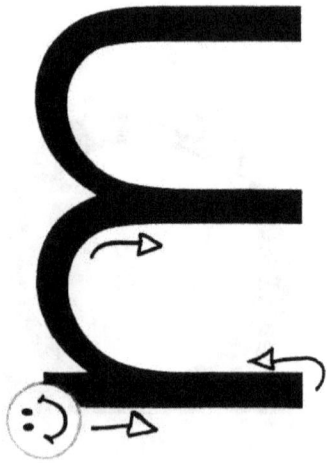

ran

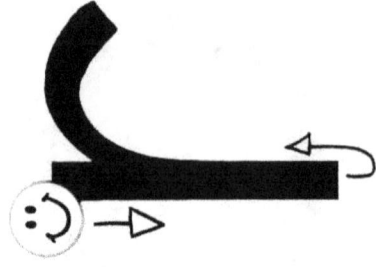

queen

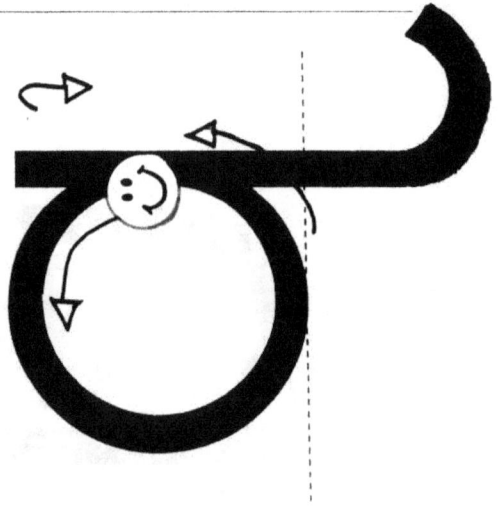

pa

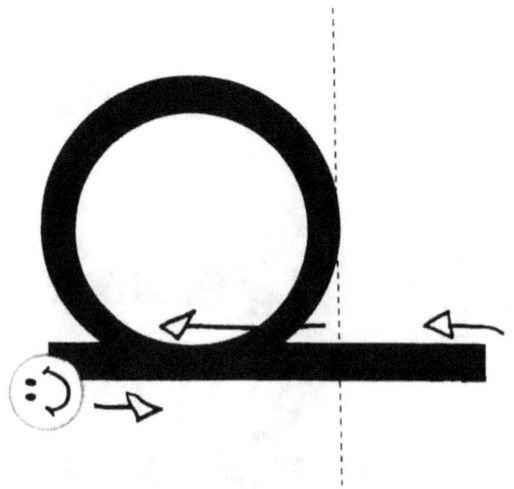

up

U

Tom talks

t

snake

s

yes! yo-yo's!

Y

zebra

Z

water

w

ax

x

valley

v

up

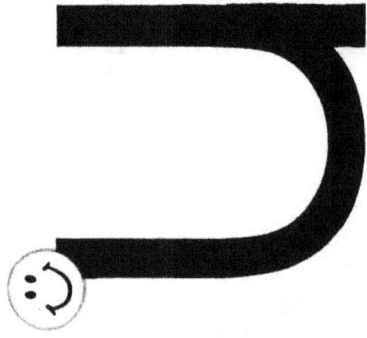

Tom talks

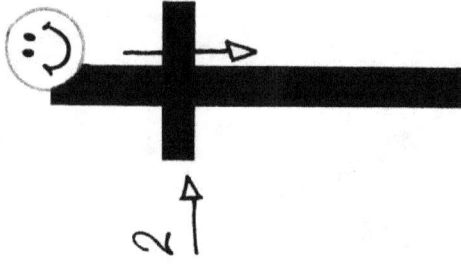

snake

yes! yo-yo's!

zebra

water

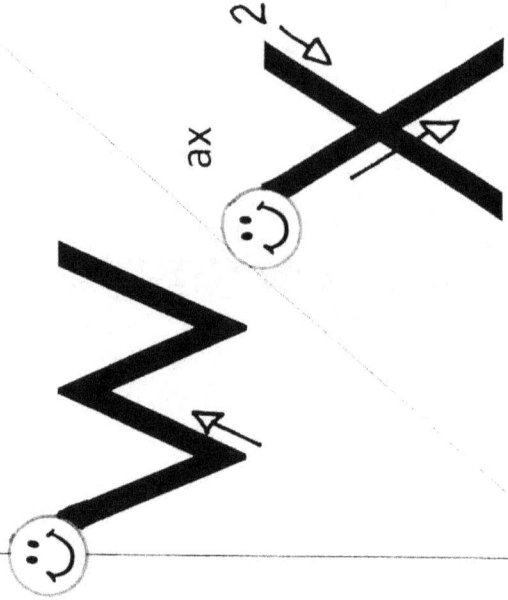

ax

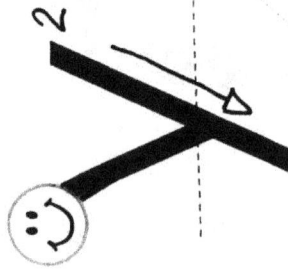

valley

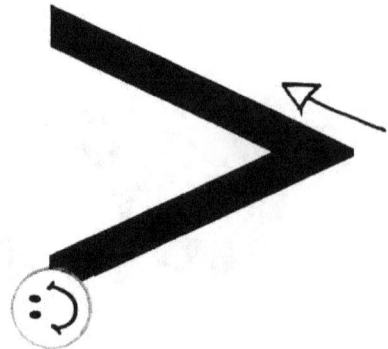

First words

i.....f — if   (if it rains)

i.....t — it   (it is daytime)

i.....s — is   (is it night-time?)

i.....n — in   (in the box)

o.....n — on   (on the table)

o.....x — ox   (an ox is big)

a.....t — at   (at the edge)

a.....x — ax   (an ax cuts trees)

a.....m — am   (I am me!)

a.....n — an   (an alligator)

a.....s — as   (as I eat, I get full)

u.....p — up   (up the valley)

a.....d — ad   (here is the ad)

u.....s — us   (we are us!)

e.....x — ex   (the letter x)

First story (2-letter words)

Now the two-letter words are put into the child's first fun reading story. There are no capital letters, because the child has not learned those yet. Slide a blank 3x5 card under each line as the child begins to read it himself, to help him keep his place. You read the entire thing to him first—with lots of expression! Once he has mastered reading the story WORDS himself, proceed to then teach him to use EXPRESSION by noting the punctuation.

is it an ox ?

it **is** an ox.

if it **is**…?

it **is**!

tis an ox.

na, tis an ax.

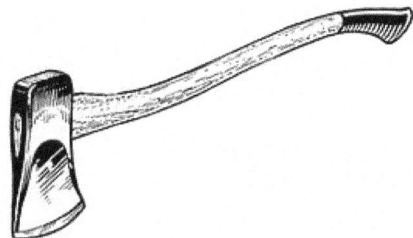

an ox it am.

if it **am** an ox, **it is** !

na, an ax it am.

if it **am** an ax, it **is** !

an ax is on an ox.

an ax is **in** an ox, it **is** !   ug !

an ex is **on** an ox.

up, ox, up !

ox, up, up !

an **ox** + an **ax** + an **ex** am
   in an in [inn].

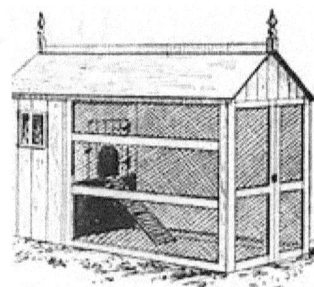

it is as it is !!!

Ready for more? This is the table of contents of the companion 180-page book, *Fast Phonics*:

6 reasons why *Fast Phonics* is more effective, more fun and more rapidly acquired than traditional phonics methods:

1

Fast Phonics gets the child **READING RIGHT NOW** (details come later).

With this revolutionary method you waste no time getting right to the core of the key skill it takes to actually read. *Fast Phonics* achieves this by teaching only the 26 PHONETIC SOUND/ SYMBOLS first. The teaching of the alphabet NAMES and capital letters is postponed until a child is already reading three-letter words.

2

The "memory hook cartoons" are meticulously crafted to deliver the **STRONGEST POSSIBLE RECALL** of each visual symbol to its sound.

The cartoons are designed to be germane to the INSIDE of the letter itself, not crafted only as novel appendages hanging all over the OUTSIDE of the letter as in other phonics programs.

3

Fast Phonics continually requires small **choices of discrimination**, so the brain HAS to stay alert at all times while doing each lesson.

The course uses frequent fun checking/testing. The child himself knows at each stage what he retains and what he does not yet retain. This method **jettisons any possibility of having a lazy brain** while gaining all of the skills necessary to read.

4

Fast Phonics uses **both hemispheres of the brain** to log in all of the material:

The visual section: initially with the cartoons—later with the exercises.

The motor planning/tactile section: initially with the no-pencil tracing (using the pointer finger only) and hand motions, and later with having to manipulate the information within all of the other skills.

5

Vowels are taught with exceptional clarity.

Short vowels are treated as "one of the boys." They are learned right along-side ordinary consonants as if they were no different. When long vowels are introduced, their conversions from short to long are drilled (nailed) 160 times before those long vowels are ever used in a sentence. Once he begins encountering these two vowel words in any new reading context, the child KNOWS how to decode them instantly.

6

Fast Phonics **builds HUMOR into the program** so that the student's emotions are happily enticed to dive into print with gusto!

www.ingramcontent.com/pod-product-compliance
Lightning Source LLC
LaVergne TN
LVHW081322060426
835509LV00015B/1636